Priests who are sad: console them, Jesus.

Priests who are worried: give them peace, Jesus.

Priest who are old: sustain them, Jesus.

Priests who are alone: accompany them, Jesus.

Missionary priests: protect them, Jesus.

Priests who are preachers: enlighten them, Jesus.

Priest who direct souls: instruct them, Jesus.

Priests and religious who have died: bring
them to glory, Jesus.

Give them your wisdom and knowledge, Jesus.

Give them your understanding and counsel, Jesus.

Give them reverence and awe of you, Jesus.

Give them patience and love, Jesus.

Give them obedience and kindness, Jesus.

Give them a burning zeal for souls, Jesus.

Give them virtues of faith, hope, and love, Jesus.

Give them an intense love for the Eucharist, Jesus.

Give them loyalty to the Holy Father and their
bishops, Jesus.

Give them respect for life and human dignity, Jesus.

Give them integrity and justice, Jesus.

Give them humility and generosity, Jesus.

Give them strength in their labors, Jesus.

Give them peace in their sufferings, Jesus.

Give them great love for the Trinity, Jesus.

Give them great love for Mary, Jesus.
Let them radiate your light, Jesus.
Let them be the salt of the earth, Jesus.
Let them practice sacrifice and self-denial, Jesus.
Let them be holy in body, mind and spirit, Jesus.
Let them be men of prayer, Jesus.
May faith shine forth in them, Jesus.
May they be concerned for our salvation, Jesus.
May they be faithful to their priestly vocation, Jesus.
May their hands bless and heal, Jesus.
May they burn with love for you, Jesus.
May all their steps be for the glory of God, Jesus.
May the Holy Spirit fill them, and give them
  his gifts in abundance, Jesus.

Let us pray:
Father, Son, and Holy Spirit, hear the prayers
we offer for our priests. Let them know clearly
the work that you are calling them to do. Grant
them every grace to answer your call with
courage, love, and lasting dedication to your
will. We ask Mary's intercession as their loving
Mother. Amen.

St. John Paul II

O Mary, Mother of Jesus Christ and Mother
of priests, accept this title which we bestow
on you to celebrate your motherhood and to
contemplate with you the Priesthood of your
Son and of your sons, O Holy Mother of God.

O Mother of Christ, to the Messiah-Priest you gave a body of flesh through the anointing of the Holy Spirit for the salvation of the poor and the contrite of heart; guard priests in your heart and in the Church, O Mother of the Saviour.

O Mother of Faith, you accompanied to the Temple the Son of Man, the fulfilment of the promises given to the fathers; give to the Father for his glory the priests of your Son, O Ark of the Covenant.

O Mother of the Church, in the midst of the disciples in the Upper Room you prayed to the Spirit for the new People and their Shepherds; obtain for the Order of Presbyters a full measure of gifts, O Queen of the Apostles.

O Mother of Jesus Christ, you were with him at the beginning of his life and mission, you sought the Master among the crowd, you stood beside him when he was lifted up from the earth consumed as the one eternal sacrifice and you had John, your son, near at hand; accept from the beginning those who have been called, protect their growth, in their life ministry accompany your sons, O Mother of Priests. Amen.

Litany of Jesus Christ, Priest and Victim

This litany was often prayed by St. John Paul II.

Lord, have mercy. *R. Lord, have mercy.*
Christ have mercy. *R. Christ, have mercy.*
Lord, have mercy. *R. Lord, have mercy.*
Christ hear us. *R. Christ, hear us.*
Christ graciously hear us. *R. Christ, graciously
  hear us.*

God the Father of Heaven, *R. Have mercy on us.*
God the Son, Redeemer of the world, *R. Have
  mercy on us.*
God the Holy Spirit *R. Have mercy on us.*
Holy Trinity, one God, *R. Have mercy on us.*

Jesus, Priest and Victim, *R. Have mercy on us.*
  Jesus, Priest forever according to the order
  of Melchizedek, *R. etc.*
Jesus, Priest whom God sent to preach the
  Gospel to the poor,
Jesus, Priest who at the Last Supper instituted
  the form of the eternal sacrifice,
Jesus, Priest who lives forever to intercede for us,
Jesus, High Priest whom the Father anointed
  with the Holy Spirit and power,
Jesus, High Priest chosen from among men,
Jesus, made High Priest for men,
Jesus, High Priest of our confession of faith,
Jesus, High Priest of greater glory than Moses,

Jesus, High Priest of the true tabernacle,

Jesus, High Priest of the good things to come,

Jesus, High Priest, holy, innocent and undefiled,

Jesus, High Priest faithful and merciful,

Jesus, High Priest inflamed with zeal for God and souls,

Jesus, High Priest, perfect forever,

Jesus, High Priest, who by your own Blood entered the heavens,

Jesus, High Priest, who opened a new way for us,

Jesus, High Priest, who loved us and washed us from our sins in your Blood,

Jesus, High Priest, who offered yourself to God as an oblation and sacrificial Victim,

Jesus, sacrificial Victim of God and men,

Jesus, holy and immaculate sacrificial Victim,

Jesus, pleasing sacrificial Victim,

Jesus, peace-making sacrificial Victim,

Jesus, sacrifice of propitiation and praise,

Jesus, sacrificial Victim of reconciliation and peace,

Jesus, sacrificial Victim in whom we have confidence and access to God,

Jesus, sacrificial Victim living forever and ever,

Be merciful, *spare us, Jesus.*
Be merciful, *graciously hear us, Jesus.*

From rashly entering the clergy, *R. deliver us, Jesus.*
From the sin of sacrilege,
From the spirit of incontinence,
From sordid pursuits,
From every lapse into simony,
From the unworthy administration of the Church's treasures,
From the love of the world and its vanities,
From the unworthy celebration of your Mysteries,
Through your eternal priesthood,
Through the holy anointing whereby you were constituted a priest by God the Father,
Through your priestly spirit,
Through that ministry whereby you glorified your Father on earth,
Through the bloody immolation of yourself made once and for all upon the Cross,
Through that same sacrifice daily renewed upon the altar,
Through that divine power which you exercise invisibly in your priests,

That you would deign to maintain the whole priestly order in holy religion, *R. We beseech you, hear us.*
That you would deign to provide your people with pastors after your own heart,

That you would deign to fill them with the
spirit of your priesthood,
That the lips of your priests might preserve
true knowledge,
That you would deign to send faithful workers
into your harvest,
That you would deign to multiply the faithful
dispensers of your Mysteries,
That you would deign to grant them
perseverance in the service of your will,
That you would deign to give them gentleness
in their ministry, resourcefullness in their
actions, and constancy in prayer,
That through them you would deign to
promote the veneration of the Blessed
Sacrament everywhere,
That you would deign to receive into your joy
those who have served you well,

Lamb of God, who takes away the sin of the
world, *spare us, O Lord.*
Lamb of God, who takes away the sin of the
world, *graciously hear us, O Lord.*
Lamb of God, who takes away the sin of the
world, *have mercy on us, O Lord.*
Jesus, Our Priest, *hear us.*
Jesus, Our Priest, *graciously hear us.*

Let us pray:

O God, Sanctifier and Guardian of your Church, raise up in her through your Spirit suitable and faithful dispensers of the holy Mysteries, so that by their ministry and example, the Christian people may be guided under your protection in the path of salvation. Through Christ our Lord. Amen.

O God, who, while the disciples were worshiping and fasting, ordered Saul and Barnabas to be set apart for the work to which you had called them, be present now to your Church in prayer, and you, who know the hearts of all, indicate those whom you have chosen for ministry. Through Christ our Lord. Amen.

For a Priest Before Mass

Almighty God, hear the prayers of your priest. In your mercy, purify him and comfort him with renewed trust in your fidelity, that he may be strengthened to fulfill the duties of the vocation you have entrusted to him. Cleanse, too, our hearts, and open our minds to receive from this priest, your servant, the words of everlasting life. Amen.

The Chaplet of St. Michael*

This chaplet is from a revelation of St. Michael the Archangel to Servant of God Sr. Antonia d'Astonac in 1751, approved by the Sacred Congregation of Rites in 1851. Pray it for your priest and an angel from each choir of the nine angelic choirs will be with him at Mass!

Oh God, come to my assistance. O Lord, make haste to help me. Glory be...

Say one Our Father and three Hail Marys after each of the following nine salutations in honor of the nine choirs of angels:

By the intercession of St. Michael and the celestial Choir of Seraphim, may the Lord make him worthy to burn with the fire of perfect charity.

By the intercession of St. Michael and the celestial Choir of Cherubim, may the Lord vouchsafe to grant him grace to leave the ways of wickedness to run in the paths of Christian perfection.

By the intercession of St. Michael and the celestial Choir of Thrones, may the Lord infuse into his heart a true and sincere spirit of humility.

By the intercession of St. Michael and the celestial Choir of Dominions, may the Lord give him grace to govern his senses and subdue his unruly passions.

By the intercession of St. Michael and the celestial Choir of Powers, may the Lord vouchsafe to protect his soul against the snares and temptations of the devil.

By the intercession of St. Michael and the celestial Choir of Virtues, may the Lord preserve him from evil and suffer him not to fall into temptation.

By the intercession of St. Michael and the celestial Choir of Principalities, may God fill his soul with a true spirit of obedience.

By the intercession of St. Michael and the celestial Choir of Archangels, may the Lord give him perseverance in faith and in all good works, in order that he gain the glory of Paradise.

By the intercession of St. Michael and the celestial Choir of Angels, may the Lord grant him to be protected by them in this mortal life and conducted hereafter to eternal glory.

Say one Our Father each in honor of the following leading angels: St. Michael, St. Gabriel, St. Raphael, Guardian Angel.

O glorious Prince St. Michael, chief and commander of the heavenly hosts, guardian of souls, vanquisher of rebel spirits, servant in the house of the Divine King, and our admirable conductor, thou who dost shine with excellence and superhuman virtue, vouchsafe to deliver Father N. from all evil, I turn to thee with confidence, and enable him by thy gracious protection to serve God more and more faithfully every day.

V. Pray for him, O glorious St. Michael, Prince of the Church of Jesus Christ. R. That he may be made worthy of the promises of Christ.

Almighty and Everlasting God, who by a prodigy of goodness and a merciful desire for the salvation of all people, hast appointed the most glorious Archangel, St. Michael, Prince of Thy Church, make Father N. worthy, we beseech Thee, to be delivered from all his enemies that none of them may harass him at the hour of death, but that he may be conducted by Thy Archangel into the august presence of Thy Divine Majesty. This we beg through the merits of Jesus Christ our Lord. Amen.

* (Adapted from 1st person to 3rd person usage.)

The Way of the Cross

With Supplemental
Prayers for Priests

ENTRANCE SONG

1. At the cross her station keep-ing
2. Through her heart His sor-row shar-ing,

1. Stood the mourn-ful Mo-ther weep-ing
2. All His bit - ter an-guish bear-ing,

1. Close to Je - sus to the last.
2. Now at length the sword had passed.

THE WAY OF THE CROSS
FOR PRIESTS

O dearest Lord Jesus, I offer Thee the way of the Cross which I am about to make for Thy honor and glory and for all Thy priests, especially those who are suffering persecution for Thy sake.

PREPARATORY PRAYER

In the name of the Father, and of the Son, and of the Holy Ghost. Amen.

In a spirit of humility and with a contrite heart, we offer unto Thee, eternal Father, this tribute of our worship, that it may redound to Thy honor and glory, and may avail us and all faithful Christians, both living and dead, unto the forgiveness of sins and the attainment of life everlasting.[1]

℣. IT BEHOOVES US TO GLORY IN THE CROSS OF OUR LORD JESUS CHRIST.

℞. IN WHOM IS OUR SALVATION, LIFE AND RESURRECTION.[2]

Let Us Pray

O God, who in the passion of Thy Son / didst show us the path to eternal glory by the way of the cross: / graciously grant that as by our prayers we now follow Him to the place of Calvary, / so we may also share His triumph with Him for all eternity. / Who liveth and reigneth with Thee for ever and ever. Amen.[3]

OH, HOW SAD AND SORE DISTRESSED
WAS THAT MOTHER HIGHLY BLESSED
OF THE SOLE-BEGOTTEN ONE!

CHRIST ABOVE IN TORMENT HANGS;
SHE BENEATH BEHOLDS THE PANGS
OF HER DYING GLORIOUS SON.

---

[1] Compiled from offertory prayers of the Mass. [2] Introit of Holy Thursday. [3] Rite of the erection of the Stations of the Cross.

FIRST STATION

Jesus Is Condemned to Death

℣. WE ADORE THEE, O CHRIST, AND WE PRAISE THEE.

℟. BECAUSE BY THY HOLY CROSS THOU HAST REDEEMED THE WORLD.[1]

And in the morning the chief priests and the whole council, binding Jesus, led Him away and delivered Him to Pilate. And they all condemned Him and said: He is guilty of death. And Pilate sat in the place of judgment and delivered Him to them to be crucified.[2]

℣. GOD SPARED NOT HIS ONLY SON.

℟. BUT DELIVERED HIM UP FOR ALL OF US.[3]

Let Us Pray

O Lord, Jesus Christ, / who didst come down to earth from the bosom of the Father in Heaven / and didst shed Thy precious blood for the remission of our sins; / we humbly beseech Thee, that on the day of judgment we may be found worthy to be on Thy right hand / and to hear Thy words: Come, ye blessed of My Father! / Who livest and reignest for ever and ever. Amen.[4]

WHO, ON CHRIST'S DEAR MOTHER GAZING
PIERCED BY ANGUISH SO AMAZING,
BORN OF WOMAN, WOULD NOT WEEP?

---

[1] Tract of Votive Mass of the Holy Cross. [2] Mk. 15:1, Mt. 26:66, and Jn. 19:16. [3] First antiphon of Lauds for Good Friday. (Rom. 8:32). [4] Collect, Votive Mass of the Passion of Our Lord.

For Priests:

Dearest Lord Jesus, I thank Thee for permitting Thyself to be unjustly condemned to death for our sakes. By this outrage I beg of Thee to grant to all priests the grace to condemn themselves by dying to the world while they are still on earth, that it may not be necessary for Thee to condemn them when they come to die. I also beg of Thee through this indignity to aid those priests who are suffering unjust condemnation for Thy sake, that they may bear their sufferings patiently in union with Thine.

SECOND STATION

Jesus Takes Up His Cross

℣. WE ADORE THEE, O CHRIST, AND WE PRAISE THEE.

℟. BECAUSE BY THY HOLY CROSS THOU HAST REDEEMED THE WORLD.

And bearing His cross He went forth to that place which is called Calvary. Hail, O Christ our King! Thou alone hast had pity on the folly of our sins. Obedient to the Father, Thou art led forth to be crucified, like an innocent lamb to the slaughter. To Thee be glory; to Thee be triumph and victory; to Thee the crown of highest honor and acclaim![1]

℣. THE LORD HATH LAID ON HIM THE INIQUITY OF US ALL.

℟. FOR THE WICKEDNESS OF HIS PEOPLE HE HATH STRICKEN HIM.[2]

Let Us Pray

O Lord, who hast said: / My yoke is sweet and My burden is light: / grant that we may be able so to carry it as to obtain Thy grace. / Who livest and reignest for ever and ever. Amen.[3]

WHO, ON CHRIST'S DEAR MOTHER THINKING,
SUCH A CUP OF SORROW DRINKING,
WOULD NOT SHARE HER SORROWS DEEP?

---

[1] Jn. 19:17 and Alleluia Verse (Paschal Time) of Votive Mass of the Passion of Our Lord. [2] Is. 53:6 and 8. [3] Vesting prayer before Mass.

For Priests:

Dearest Lord Jesus, I thank Thee for taking the rough cross upon Thy wounded shoulders and bearing it to Calvary. By Thy humble acceptance of the cross I beg of Thee to grant to priests the grace to accept humbly the crosses of their vocation. I ask of Thee also to grant to those priests, who are forced by Thy enemies and theirs to bear the many crosses of persecution, to follow courageously in Thy bloody footprints.

THIRD STATION

Jesus Falls the First Time Under the Cross

℣. WE ADORE THEE, O CHRIST, AND WE PRAISE THEE.

℟. BECAUSE BY THY HOLY CROSS THOU HAST REDEEMED THE WORLD.

Our Lord Jesus Christ humbled Himself unto death, even to the death of the cross. For which cause God hath exalted Him and hath given Him a name that is above every name. Come, let us adore and bow down before God, let us weep in the presence of the Lord who made us, for He is indeed the Lord our God.[1]

℣. SURELY HE HATH BORNE OUR INFIRMITIES.

℟. AND HE HATH CARRIED OUR SORROWS.[2]

Let Us Pray

Grant, we beseech Thee, almighty God, / that we, who fail in so many adversities through our own weakness, / may take heart again through the pleading of the passion of Thine only-begotten Son. / Who liveth and reigneth for ever and ever. Amen.[3]

BRUISED, DERIDED, CURSED, DEFILED,
SHE BEHELD HER TENDER CHILD
ALL WITH BLOODY SCOURGES RENT.

---

[1] Epistle of Palm Sunday (Philip. 2:8-9) and Ps. 94:6-7 of daily Matins. [2] Is. 53:4. [3] Collect, Monday in Holy Week.

For Priests:

My dearest Jesus, I thank Thee for this first time when Thou didst stumble and fall beneath Thy cross. By the humiliation Thou didst suffer here I beg of Thee to grant to priests the grace of avoiding all deliberate sin and, should they be so unfortunate as to fall, to rise at once and continue following after Thee. Grant also, dearest Jesus, to those who suffer persecution for thy sake the grace to follow Thee unceasingly without regard to human respect.

FOURTH STATION

Jesus Meets His Afflicted Mother

℣.   WE ADORE THEE, O CHRIST, AND WE PRAISE THEE.

℞.   BECAUSE BY THY HOLY CROSS THOU HAST REDEEMED THE WORLD.

To what shall I compare thee; or to what shall I liken thee, O virgin daughter of Jerusalem? For great as the sea is thy distress. O Mother of mercy, grant that we may ever realize in ourselves the death of Jesus and may share with Him in His saving passion.[1]

℣.   A SWORD OF SORROW HATH PIERCED THY SOUL.

℞.   AND HATH FILLED THY HEART WITH BITTER PAIN.[2]

Let Us Pray

O Lord Jesus Christ, / grant that now and in the hour of our death / we may obtain the favor of Thy mercy / through the pleading of the Blessed Virgin Mary, Thy Mother, / whose soul was pierced with a sword of sorrow in the hour of Thy passion. / Who livest and reignest for ever and ever. Amen.[3]

O THOU MOTHER, FONT OF LOVE,
TOUCH MY SPIRIT FROM ABOVE,
MAKE MY HEART WITH THINE ACCORD.

---

[1] Lam. of Jer. 2:13 and *Stabat Mater*. [2] Lk. 2:35 and Job 9:18.
[3] Collect, Votive Mass of the Seven Sorrows of the B.V.M.

For Priests:

My dearest Lord Jesus, I thank Thee for this heart-rending meeting on thy journey to Calvary. Through the union of Thy Most Sacred Heart with the Heart of Thy Immaculate Mother I beg of Thee to give Thy priests the grace to have Mary as their most powerful aid and comfort in life and at the hour of death. Grant also, O dearest Jesus, that Thy sweetest Mother may, in a special manner, be with those priests who are suffering persecution for Thy sake. May she comfort them in their hour of trial and darkness as she comforted Thee on Thy way to execution.

FIFTH STATION

Simon of Cyrene Is Forced to Take Up the Cross

℣. WE ADORE THEE. O CHRIST. AND WE PRAISE THEE.

℟. BECAUSE BY THY HOLY CROSS THOU HAST REDEEMED THE WORLD.

And as they led Him away, they laid hold of one Simon of Cyrene, a passer-by, and forced him to take up the cross of Jesus. And they laid the cross on him, to carry after Jesus.[1]

℣. WHOEVER DOES NOT CARRY HIS CROSS AND COME AFTER ME.

℟. CANNOT BE MY DISCIPLE.[2]

Let Us Pray

Receive our prayers, O Lord, / and be appeased, / and in Thy mercy subdue to Thy service even our rebellious wills. / Through Christ our Lord. Amen.[3]

FOR THE SINS OF HIS OWN NATION,
SAW HIM HANG IN DESOLATION,
TILL HIS SPIRIT FORTH HE SENT.

---

[1] Mt. 27:32, Mk. 15:21, and Lk. 23:26. [2] Lk. 14:27. [3] Secret, Saturday of Fourth Week in Lent.

For Priests:

Dearest Lord Jesus, I thank Thee for permitting this small aid to be given Thee, even by one who was unwilling to render Thee a service. By the help Thou didst accept from Simon, I beseech Thee to send to Thy priests someone to advise, encourage and support them, someone to aid them in moments of suffering, when the crosses of their vocation become almost too heavy to bear alone. Give also to those priests who bear the cross of persecution and torture the grace of a helping hand, a consoling voice, a deed of kindness, that in their most discouraged moments they may know that Thou art with them, sharing their crosses as they share Thine.

SIXTH STATION

Veronica Wipes the Face of Jesus

℣. WE ADORE THEE, O CHRIST, AND WE PRAISE THEE.

℟. BECAUSE BY THY HOLY CROSS THOU HAST REDEEMED THE WORLD.

Lo, we have seen Him, and there is no beauty in Him nor comeliness; He is despised and the most abject of men, a man of sorrows and acquainted with infirmity. His countenance is as it were hidden, whereupon we esteemed Him not. His appearance is inglorious among men, and His form among the children of men. And yet He is the beautiful one above all the sons of men, and by His bruises we are healed.[1]

℣. TURN NOT THY FACE AWAY FROM US.

℟. AND WITHDRAW NOT FROM THY SERVANTS IN THINE ANGER.[2]

Let Us Pray

O God, who dost renew us to Thine image / by the precious blood of Jesus Christ Thy Son: / lead our footsteps in Thy paths, / so that we may truly obtain the gift of Thy divine charity. / Through the same Christ our Lord. Amen.[3]

MAKE ME FEEL AS THOU HAST FELT;
MAKE MY SOUL TO GLOW AND MELT
WITH THE LOVE OF CHRIST MY LORD.

---

[1] Third Responsory, Tenebrae of Holy Thursday, Is. 53:3, 52:14, Ps. 44:3. [2] Ps. 26:9. [3] Secret "For Charity."

For Priests:

My sweetest Lord, I thank Thee for leaving the image of thy most holy and adorable face upon Veronica's veil. By this most gracious reward to Veronica, I beg of Thee to grant to all priests the grace of recognizing Thy holy image in themselves and in those entrusted to their care. I beg of Thee also, O most sweet Jesus, to grant to those priests who are suffering persecution to recognize Thy image, however disfigured, in their persecutors that they, too, may develop Thy image in themselves by dying with a prayer of forgiveness and love for their enemies on their lips.

SEVENTH STATION

Jesus Falls a Second Time

℣.   WE ADORE THEE, O CHRIST, AND WE PRAISE THEE.

℞.   BECAUSE BY THY HOLY CROSS THOU HAST REDEEMED THE WORLD.

They delivered Me into the hands of the impious, they cast Me out amongst the wicked, and they spared not My soul. The powerful gathered together against Me, and like giants they stood against Me. And striking Me with cruel wounds, they mocked Me.[1]

℣.   BUT I AM A WORM AND NO MAN.
℞.   THE REPROACH OF MEN AND THE OUT-CAST OF THE PEOPLE.[2]

Let Us Pray

O God, who by the humility of Thy Son hast lifted up a fallen world: / grant to Thy faithful people abiding joy; / that those whom Thou hast delivered from the perils of eternal death, / may come to enjoy unending happiness. / Through the same Christ our Lord. Amen.[3]

HOLY MOTHER, PIERCE ME THROUGH.
IN MY HEART EACH WOUND RENEW
OF MY SAVIOUR CRUCIFIED.

LET ME SHARE WITH THEE HIS PAIN,
WHO FOR ALL MY SINS WAS SLAIN,
WHO FOR ME IN TORMENTS DIED.

---

[1] Seventh Responsory, Tenebrae of Good Friday, First Responsory, *ibid.* [2] Ps. 21:7. [3] Collect, Second Sunday after Easter.

For Priests:

My dearest Lord Jesus, I thank Thee for this second most painful fall. By the bruises Thou didst suffer when for the second time the cross bore Thee to the ground, I beseech Thee to grant to all priests the grace of fidelity to their duty as shepherds of souls. Let such as fall from the ideals of their state of life, O Lord, profit by Thy rising from Thy second fall, and rising, too, continue to follow after Thee. Grant also, O my Jesus, to those who are tempted to shirk their priestly duties for fear of persecution, to take courage from Thy falls and bear their crosses faithfully in union with Thee.

EIGHTH STATION

Jesus Meets the Women of Jerusalem

℣. WE ADORE THEE, O CHRIST, AND WE PRAISE THEE.

℞. BECAUSE BY THY HOLY CROSS THOU HAST REDEEMED THE WORLD.

And there followed Him a great multitude of people and of women who bewailed and lamented Him. But Jesus turning to them said: Daughters of Jerusalem, weep not over Me, but weep for yourselves and for your children.[1]

℣. THEY THAT SOW IN TEARS.

℞. SHALL REAP IN JOY.[2]

Let Us Pray

O God, who dost choose rather to have mercy / than to be angry with those who hope in Thee: / grant that we may truly grieve for the evil we have done, / and so deserve to obtain the grace of Thy consolation. / Through Christ our Lord. Amen.[3]

LET ME MINGLE TEARS WITH THEE,
MOURNING HIM WHO MOURNED FOR ME,
ALL THE DAYS THAT I MAY LIVE.

---

[1] Lk. 23:27-28. [2] Ps. 125:5. [3] Prayer for the People, Saturday of Fourth Week in Lent.

For Priests:

My dearest Jesus, I thank Thee for the consolation Thou didst give to these women who bewailed Thy sufferings. Grant, O dearest Lord, to all Thy priests, the grace of being merciful and kind to all who need their aid. Give them patience, understanding, and sympathy with all who suffer that their priestly hearts may reflect the virtues of Thy Own great Heart. To those who suffer trials and torments for Thy sake, give O Lord, the grace so that, in imitation of Thee, they may not permit their pains to make them unmindful of the pains of others.

NINTH STATION

Jesus Falls a Third Time

℣. WE ADORE THEE, O CHRIST, AND WE PRAISE THEE.

℟. BECAUSE BY THY HOLY CROSS THOU HAST REDEEMED THE WORLD.

My people, what have I done to thee, or in what have I grieved thee? Answer Me. I brought thee out of the land of Egypt, and thou hast led Me to the gibbet of the cross. Forty years I fed thee with manna in the desert, and thou hast beaten Me with blows and scourges. What more ought I do for thee that I have not done?[1]

℣. HE WAS LED AS A SHEEP TO THE SLAUGHTER.

℟. AND HE WAS MUTE AS A LAMB BEFORE THE SHEARER.[2]

Let Us Pray

Guard us, we beseech Thee, O Lord, / in Thy ever-present mercy; / and since without Thee weak man must fail, / keep us ever by Thy help from all things harmful, / and lead us to all things profitable unto our salvation. / Through Christ our Lord. Amen.[3]

BY THE CROSS WITH THEE TO STAY;
THERE WITH THEE TO WEEP AND PRAY;
THIS I ASK OF THEE TO GIVE.

---

[1] Reproaches of Good Friday. [2] Is. 53:7. [3] Collect, Fourteenth Sunday after Pentecost.

For Priests:

I thank Thee, dear Lord Jesus, for the third time when Thy sacred Body was pressed to the earth through the weight of Thy sufferings. By Thy fearless courage in rising from this third most painful fall, grant, O Jesus, to all Thy priests the grace to be faithful to their vocations forever, and to those who have turned their backs on Thee, give the humility to return to Thee, rising from their fall, assured that Thou wilt receive them once again into Thy friendship. I beg especially, O blessed Jesus, the grace of fortitude for those priests who live in danger of persecution. Give them the courage to adhere to Thee regardless of threats or violence; keep them for Thyself alone, and move the hearts of the apostates to rise from their defection and once more take up their crosses and follow after Thee.

TENTH STATION

Jesus Is Stripped of His Garments

℣. WE ADORE THEE, O CHRIST, AND WE PRAISE THEE.

℟. BECAUSE BY THY HOLY CROSS THOU HAST REDEEMED THE WORLD.

And they came to the place that is called Golgotha, which is the place of Calvary. And they gave Him wine to drink, mingled with gall. And when He had tasted, He would not drink. And they divided His garments, casting lots; that it might be fulfilled which was spoken by the prophet, saying: They divided My garments among them; and upon My vesture they cast lots.[1]

℣. THEY GAVE ME GALL FOR MY FOOD.
℟. AND IN MY THIRST THEY GAVE ME VINEGAR TO DRINK.[2]

Let Us Pray

Strip us, O Lord, of our former self / with its evil deeds and ways; / and clothe us with that new nature which is created after the manner of God / in justice and in holiness of truth. / Through Christ our Lord. Amen.[3]

VIRGIN, OF ALL VIRGINS BLEST!
LISTEN TO MY FOND REQUEST:
LET ME SHARE THY GRIEF WITH THEE.

---

[1] Mt. 27:33-35. [2] Ps. 68:22. [3] Rite of religious profession.

For Priests:

O dearest Lord, I thank Thee for the shame and humiliation which Thou didst endure when Thou didst permit Thyself to be stripped of Thy clothing on Calvary. My purest Jesus, by this great indignity, I beseech Thee to give to Thy priests great purity of heart and intention in serving Thee, and likewise the grace and courage to strip themselves of all things which are in any way displeasing to thee. Look in pity, also, on those priests, who, like Thee, are stripped of all their possessions and whose dignity and sanctity of person are disregarded by their persecutors. Help them, O loving Jesus, to unite their humiliations to Thee.

ELEVENTH STATION

Jesus Is Nailed to the Cross

℣.   WE ADORE THEE, O CHRIST, AND WE PRAISE THEE.

℟.   BECAUSE BY THY HOLY CROSS THOU HAST REDEEMED THE WORLD.

And when they were come to the place which is called Calvary, they crucified Him there, and with Him two thieves, one on the right and the other on the left, and Jesus in the midst. My people, what have I done to thee? I have exalted thee with great power, and thou hast hanged Me on the gibbet of the cross.[1]

℣.   THEY HAVE PIERCED MY HANDS AND FEET.

℟.   THEY HAVE NUMBERED ALL MY BONES.[2]

Let Us Pray

O God, who by the passion of Thine only-begotten Son, / and by the five wounds from which His blood was poured, / didst repair the evil wrought by sin in our human nature: / grant, we beseech Thee, / that we who here on earth revere the wounds which He received, / may be worthy to obtain in Heaven the fruit of His most precious blood. / Through the same Christ our Lord. Amen.[3]

> LET ME TO MY LATEST BREATH,
> IN MY BODY BEAR THE DEATH
> OF THAT DYING SON OF THINE.

---

[1] Lk. 23:33, Jn. 19:18 and Reproaches of Good Friday. [2] Ps. 21:17-18. [3] Collect, Feast of the Five Wounds.

For Priests:

Dearest Lord Jesus, I thank Thee for giving Thyself into the hands of Thy executioners to be crucified and for the example of heroic patience which Thou didst give us in Thy terrible agony. I beg of Thee, my sweetest Lord, by Thy great pains to grant to all of Thy priests the grace of patience in time of trial and adversity. Especially to those chosen sons of Thine who share in the fullest sense in Thy crucifixion grant, O Lord, the grace to unite their spiritual, mental, and physical sufferings to Thine on the cross.

TWELFTH STATION

Jesus Dies on the Cross

℣. WE ADORE THEE, O CHRIST, AND WE PRAISE THEE.

℟. BECAUSE BY THY HOLY CROSS THOU HAST REDEEMED THE WORLD.

When Jesus therefore had seen His mother and the disciple whom He loved, He said to His mother: Woman, behold thy son. After that He saith to the disciple: Behold thy mother. And Jesus, when He had taken the vinegar, said: It is consummated. And again, crying with a loud voice, He said: Father, into Thy hands I commend My spirit. And bowing His head, He gave up the ghost.[1]

℣. CHRIST FOR OUR SAKE BECAME OBEDIENT UNTO DEATH.

℟. EVEN THE DEATH OF THE CROSS.[2]

Let Us Pray

O Lord Jesus Christ, Son of the living God, / who at the sixth hour didst mount the gibbet of the cross for the redemption of the world, / and didst shed Thy precious blood for the remission of our sins: / grant us, we humbly beseech Thee, / that after our death we may enter with joy the gates of Paradise. / Who livest and reignest for ever and ever. Amen.[3]

LET HIS STRIPES AND SCOURGING SMITE ME,
AT HIS HOLY CROSS REQUITE ME,
LET HIS BLOOD REFRESH ME THERE.

---

[1] Jn. 19:26, 27, and 30 and Lk. 23:46 (Fifth Responsory of Tenebrae of Good Friday). [2] Versicle of Good Friday (Philip. 2:8). [3] Postcommunion, Votive Mass of the Passion of Our Lord.

For Priests:

My Lord and my God! I love Thee with all my heart and I thank Thee for redeeming the world by giving Thy life - Thy All - for us. Jesus! I beg Thee to grant to Thy priests the grace to share in Thy all-embracing charity and to be ready to sacrifice themselves in imitation of Thee in order to further Thy Kingdom upon earth. Grant, O Jesus, that those priests who are suffering persecution for Thy sake, may ever keep in mind Thy crucifixion and death. May their love for Thee and Thine for them sustain them in their trials that they may share with Thee, not only Thy pains and sufferings, but also the triumph of Thy Resurrection!

THIRTEENTH STATION

The Body of Jesus Is Placed in the Arms of His Mother

℣. WE ADORE THEE, O CHRIST, AND WE PRAISE THEE.

℟. BECAUSE BY THY HOLY CROSS THOU HAST REDEEMED THE WORLD.

O all ye that pass by the way, stop, and consider if there be any sorrow like to my sorrow. Mine eyes have failed with weeping; my whole being is troubled, and my strength is poured out upon the earth, as I behold the cruel death of my Son, for the enemy hath prevailed against Him. Call me not Noemi (that is, beautiful), but call me Mara (that is, bitter), for the Almighty hath quite filled me with bitterness.[1]

℣. THE TEARS ARE ON HER CHEEKS.

℟. AND THERE IS NONE TO COMFORT HER.[2]

Let Us Pray

O God, at whose passion, as Simeon had foretold, / a sword of sorrow pierced the sweet soul of Mary, the glorious Virgin Mother: / grant that we, who reverently recall her anguish and suffering, / may obtain the blessed fruits of Thy redemption. / Who livest and reignest for ever and ever. Amen.[3]

WHEN THE FLAMES OF HELL WOULD END ME AT THE JUDGMENT DAY, DEFEND ME, GENTLE VIRGIN, WITH THY PRAYER.

---

[1] Lam. of Jer. 1:12, 2:11, 1-16, Ruth 1:20. [2] Lam. of Jer. 1:2.
[3] Collect, Feast of the Seven Sorrows of the B.V.M.

For Priests:

My dearest Lord, I thank Thee for resting, at Thy death as at Thy birth, in the holy arms of the Immaculate Virgin Mary. Dear Jesus, by the embrace which Thy Mother gave Thy tireless Body, grant that all Thy priests may so live as to merit being presented to Thee at the hour of their death in the arms of Thy priceless Mother. O Jesus and Mary, be at the side of all those priests who are suffering for the Faith. Grant that their torments and deaths may be but the planting of the seed from which the Church shall grow stronger and holier day by day.

FOURTEENTH STATION

Jesus Is Laid in the Tomb

℣. WE ADORE THEE, O CHRIST, AND WE PRAISE THEE.

℟. BECAUSE BY THY HOLY CROSS THOU HAST REDEEMED THE WORLD.

And Joseph, having taken down the body of Jesus, wrapped it up in a clean linen cloth, and laid it in his own new tomb which he had hewn out in a rock. And he rolled a great stone to the door of the tomb.[1]

℣. THOU WILT NOT LEAVE MY SOUL IN HELL.

℟. NOR WILT THOU GIVE THY HOLY ONE TO SEE CORRUPTION.[2]

Let Us Pray

O God, who hast left us a record of Thy passion in the holy shroud, / wherein Joseph wrapped Thy sacred body when taken down from the cross: / mercifully grant that through Thy death and burial / we may be brought to the glory of Thy resurrection. / Who livest and reignest for ever and ever. Amen.[3]

CHRIST, WHEN THOU SHALT CALL ME HENCE,
BE THY MOTHER MY DEFENSE,
BE THY CROSS MY VICTORY.

WHILE MY BODY HERE DECAYS,
MAY MY SOUL THY GOODNESS PRAISE,
SAFE IN PARADISE WITH THEE.

---

[1] Mt. 27:59-60. [2] Ps. 15:10. [3] Collect, Feast of the Holy Shroud

For Priests:

O Jesus, I thank Thee for the lessons Thou didst teach us in Thy life and by Thy death, and for the glorious Resurrection from this tomb to a life in Heaven, which we, too, hope, by Thy grace to share one day with Thee. For all Thy priests, O sweetest Lord, I beg the grace, through Thy burial to keep themselves apart from the spirit of the world even while they live in the midst of the world, and the gift, at their life's end, of final perseverance. Grant, O Lord, to all, and in a special manner to those priests who have descended for Thy sake into the dark tomb of persecution, unending happiness with Thee in Heaven. May their wounds shine resplendently in Heaven. May they be united to Thee in the perfect union of the Beatific Vision - Thy promised reward to them for sharing Thy cross here on earth.

CONCLUDING PRAYER

Let Us Pray

I thank Thee, dearest Lord Jesus, for permitting me to accompany Thee on Thy sorrowful journey to Calvary. Bless me from Thy cross and help me to love Thee more and more so that I, too, may share Heaven with Thee and with all those for whom I have prayed.

O God, who in order to drive far from us the power of the enemy, didst will that Thy Son should suffer for us on the cross: grant, we beseech Thee, that we who rejoice in honoring that same holy cross, may likewise everywhere rejoice in Thy loving care and obtain the grace of resurrection. Through the same Christ our Lord. Amen.

O Mary, Mother of Jesus, you were with Jesus at the beginning of His life and mission. You stood beside Jesus when He was lifted on the cross and gave His life for all. We ask you now to be with our priests, who give themselves in service to God's people. Intercede for them that they may grow in holiness, proclaim God's word with courage, celebrate the Sacraments with joy, and be among God's people as Jesus, the Good Shepherd, was. We offer this prayer to God, the Father, through your intercession, in the name of your Son, Jesus, and through the power of the Holy Spirit. Amen.

Psalm 116

Praise the Lord, all you nations,
  sing his glory, all you peoples.
For he has proven to us his loving-kindness,
  the Lord is true to his word forever.
Glory be the Father and to the Son,
  and to the Holy Spirit.
As it was in the beginning, is now, and ever shall be, world without end. Amen!

Without the priest, there is simply no Catholic Church. ~ St. John Paul II